DADGAD and DGDGCD

More Traditional Irish and Original Tunes and Songs

Arranged for Fingerstyle Guitar

by Julie Henigan

1 2 3 4 5 6 7 8 9 0

Visit us on the Web at www.melbay.com — E-mail us at email@melbay.com

CONTENTS

Dancing a Jig

PREFACE

In my first guitar book, *DADGAD Tuning*, I stated that the discovery of DADGAD had changed my musical life. Before I discovered this tuning, I had played folk, blues, and classical repertoire in standard tuning. My first non-standard tuning on the guitar was in fact lute tuning, in which the G string is tuned down to F♯ and a capo placed on the third fret. I later experimented with some of the more common blues open tunings, especially D and G.

But DADGAD opened up to me a whole new world of melodic and harmonic possibilities, especially in the realm of traditional Irish music, to which it is so admirably suited. I soon found that playing in DADGAD I could adapt much of the ornamentation I used in my fiddle playing to the guitar and thus render Irish tunes with unusual fidelity. And, since the tuning lends itself equally well to melodic and chordal styles of playing, I have also found it extremely effective for accompanying traditional Irish, Scottish, and English songs. While standard tuning has its own virtues where Irish music is concerned—particularly for backing instrumental tunes in a session or live performances—DADGAD (and related tunings) have made the music fall into place for me as a solo guitarist and song accompanist. Some DADGAD players have transcended the basic harmonic structure of the tuning, adding everything from thirds to major sevenths in order to play jazz standards and New Age originals. My preference, however, at least in playing traditional Irish music, is for the greater tonal indeterminacy afforded by both the modal and suspended chords integral to such tunings. I also tend to be a minimalist, using bass notes primarily as drones and harmonic ballast and only occasionally for harmonic coloring. Because of this preference, guitarists with a strong melodic bias will probably have the greatest affinity for these arrangements.

My second book is intended to provide more instrumentals and songs for those who would like to explore DADGAD further, as well as to introduce a related tuning, DGCGCD, which I describe in greater detail in the introduction. It, too, works well with a number of Irish tunes and songs, and I hope you will enjoy exploring it. I have also included more songs in this book than in my first, partly because I often include instrumentals in my arrangements of songs and also because I have received requests for my arrangements of specific songs.

I would like to emphasize that I offer this book, as I offered my previous one, as a starting point: a means by which the guitarist can gain sufficient familiarity with the tuning to proceed comfortably to further individual exploration and interpretation. Thus, while the arrangements included in this volume have been arrived at after much thought and experimentation, they are not set in stone. An arrangement is only an individual solution to a problem which can be approached from a variety of angles, and I encourage guitarists who use this book to experiment with their own solutions to setting these and any other compositions they may wish to play.

I should also mention that not all of the versions of dance tunes I have included will be note-for-note what the reader may have heard or seen elsewhere, on recordings, in sessions, other books, etc. This is because I learn many of my tunes from individuals, who may themselves possess an atypical version of the tune; because of the variability of tune versions in the tradition generally; and because of modifications I may have consciously or unconsciously made to the versions as I learned them. None of these is necessarily either right or wrong, and I hope my settings will provide you with the basic structure of the tune, which you can of course alter to suit your own musical preferences.

The majority of the selections in this book are traditional Irish dance tunes, airs, and songs, but I have also included a traditional American reel, a selection of my own tunes, and compositions by guitarist Gilles le Bigot, banjo-player Fred Boyce, and accordion-player Jake Schumacher. Some of the pieces are more difficult than others, but all should be accessible to musicians with at least an advanced beginning to intermediate knowledge of guitar technique. Some of the techniques I illustrate in this book—particularly in the execution of ornaments— will probably be unfamiliar to those with no background in Irish music. If these ornaments seem difficult at first, you can of course omit them, although with practice they should be become manageable.

As I mentioned in my first book, the importance of using one's "ear" when learning and interpreting music cannot be overstressed. My own guitar playing has been influenced by constant listening to a broad range of music—and in the case of DADGAD and DGDGCD —especially to traditional music, performed on a variety of instruments. It has also been greatly influenced by the playing of other guitarists, whose own approaches to playing in open tunings I have variously imitated, adapted, integrated, and rejected in the course of developing my own style. Because I believe that exposure to a variety of styles is essential to an individual's musical development, I have included a bibliography/discography in the back of this book, which I hope will give readers additional sources of musical ideas and inspiration.

Some of the tunes and song accompaniments in this book are built around chord positions. For this reason—and so that guitarists will be tempted to explore more of the chordal possibilities of the tuning—I have included a number of charts at the back of the book, which will provide not only an easy means of learning chord positions and patterns, but will also give the reader a representation of the harmonic structure of the tunings.

INTRODUCTION

In this introduction I will give examples of some of the techniques I use when playing in DADGAD and DGDGCD, as well as explanations of the symbols and notation used in the transcriptions in this book. First, however, I would like to present a brief history of both tunings and discuss the characteristics that give them their unique sounds.

The Development of DADGAD

The invention of DADGAD is usually attributed to English guitar virtuoso Davey Graham. Graham's extremely eclectic style and repertoire, which included classical, Renaissance, and Middle Eastern music, as well as American blues and traditional Irish dance music, significantly influenced other guitarists of his generation and established him in the forefront of what became known as the "folk baroque" style. Apparently, Graham initially developed DADGAD in the early 1960s in order to more easily accompany Moroccan *oud* players. A number of his contemporaries in England (including John Renbourn and Bert Jansch) quickly adapted the tuning to a broad range of material, including blues, medieval music, and original songs, and Martin Carthy used it as the starting point for the development of several of his own highly inventive tunings. Richard Thompson, whose repertoire has ranged from traditional Irish and English material to rock and roll, has also used DADGAD extensively throughout his career. The tuning reached what is arguably its highest level of technical complexity and musical expression in the playing of Pierre Bensusan, a brilliant and exceptionally versatile French guitarist, who, while initially using DADGAD solely for Irish and French traditional material, eventually adapted it to his own highly distinctive composition style. Other contemporary instrumentalists who have followed in Bensusan's wake are New Age guitarist Michael Hedges and Italian guitarist Peppino D'Agostino. The tuning has also gained increasing popularity in the past few years with singer-songwriters throughout the United States and Europe.

DADGAD remains, however, first and foremost, the tuning of choice for performers of traditional music, particularly what is often called traditional "Celtic music" (a term at first applied chiefly to the music of Ireland, Scotland, and Brittany, although now frequently used to include certain kinds of New Age music, as well as the music of "Celtic" enclaves in southern Europe, including Asturia). Some of the most highly regarded DADGAD guitarists in this genre (besides those already mentioned) are the late Mícheál Ó Domhnaill (formerly of the Bothy Band, but also known for his work with the Windham Hill ensemble Nightnoise), Dáithí Sproule (known most recently for his work with traditional Irish group Altan), and Breton guitarists including Soïg Siberil, Gilles le Bigot, and Nicolas Quemener.

Some Technical Considerations

DADGAD

DADGAD is what guitar players call an "open tuning." This means that the strings are tuned so that they produce a chord when sounded "open," or unfretted. The earliest open tunings were developed by blues guitarists and proved particularly effective in slide guitar playing. All of these tunings are in major keys, e.g. C, D, E, and G, the open chord thus consisting of the root, third, and fifth of each respective key (with some notes doubled). DADGAD and its near relatives, however, are in what are known as "suspended tunings," in which the chords produced omit the third interval of the chord and add one or more other notes of the scale, usually the second or the fourth. In DADGAD, the third (F♯) is omitted and the fourth (G) added. The absence of the third (which in a regular chord determines whether the chord is major or minor, depending on whether the third itself is major or minor) gives the tuning an ambiguity which can be extremely effective; while the presence of the fourth gives the tuning its evocative, "airy" quality. Because of the number of consonant open strings in DADGAD, the guitarist can also obtain what is often described as a "harp-like" effect by sounding several strings consecutively and letting them ring simultaneously. The playing of melodies with such ringing tones (and overtones) is especially effective.

The omission of the third in DADGAD is one of the characteristics that make it so appropriate for traditional music, much of which is modal. The term "modal" has been the subject of much debate and redefinition over the centuries, but in traditional music the term is generally used to refer to scales or melody types other than the major and minor scales so characteristic of Western art music since the Baroque period. These alternative scales are familiar to mountain dulcimer players, who must alter the tuning of their instruments to accommodate melodies composed in these modes. Modal folk melodies (usually determined by their final notes) feature variable scale steps, most frequently the third, seventh, and fourth. If the seventh is altered, it is often lowered (as in the so-called Dorian and Mixolydian modes). The omission of the third in an open tuning allows the guitarist to accommodate these unaccustomed tonal ambiguities and flat sevenths—in large part by failing to define the chord as major and minor, with all the attendant harmonic and melodic conventions such scales imply.

The purest modal guitar tunings are those which include only the root and fifth of a chord. These tunings function much like a dulcimer with its single melody string and two drone strings tuned a fifth apart. A number of guitarists who play Scottish and Irish music prefer such tunings—favoring those in C and G—to DADGAD, which also possesses the fourth (G). In DADGAD, the bass strings (tuned a fifth apart) still function as drones, but the inclusion of the fourth adds tone color, offering a harmonic dimension to a melody which, while not inherent in the melody itself, is compatible with it. Of course, the fourth can be excluded and the chord rendered modal; equally, the third can be added to render the chord either major or minor. Herein lies the secret of DADGAD's versatility: it can be used to play a modal melody or counter-melody with bass drones or—as in standard tuning—to play more harmonic pieces with independent parts. It is this very versatility which made the tuning so attractive to those who developed the "folk baroque" style and led to its application to tunes ranging from folk melodies to lute compositions.

DGDGCD

Unlike DADGAD, the invention or popularization of the DGDGCD tuning is not attributed to any single guitarist. Many see it as a derivation from the modal banjo tuning sometimes called "sawmill tuning" (GDGCD); and a number of guitarists (including, for example, Bill Shute) do seem to have adapted it from the banjo. However, it is also one of a family of suspended chord tunings associated with DADGAD, and has been used by many of the great British DADGAD players, including John Renbourn, Martin Carthy, and Martin Simpson, as well as by continental and American guitarists like Pierre Bensuan, Steve Baughman, and Dave Surette.

Like DADGAD, DGDGCD is a suspended fourth tuning, although this time in the key of G rather than D, a fact that is somewhat obscured by the D bass. However, as in DADGAD, the root and fifth (G and D) are doubled, the third (B) is omitted, and the fourth (C) added.

It's easy to see how experimentation with suspended tunings, as opposed to adaptation from the banjo, could lead to this modification, as my own story will illustrate. A number of years ago, a fellow musician showed me the almost identical CGDGCD tuning, in which the C bass emphasizes the presence of the fourth and, in fact, makes it easy to play "out of" C, as well as G. This tuning also creates an ethereal harmonic texture, but I found it better suited to original and contemporary instrumentals and song accompaniments than to traditional material. I then discovered that by raising the C to D, I could play more strictly in G, emphasizing the fourth less for harmonic effect and more as part of the melody. Changing the C to D also eliminates the possibility of unwanted fourth overtones in the bass.

Tuning

DADGAD

To tune into DADGAD from standard tuning (EADGBE), lower your first and sixth (top and bottom) strings a whole step from E to D. Then lower your second string a whole step from B to A. The seventh fret of the sixth string should now match the A of your open fifth string, the second fret of the third string the A of your second string, and the fifth fret of the second fret should match the D of your first string. Alternatively, you can simply tune your sixth and first strings to match the D of your open fourth string and your second string to match the A of your open fifth string.

DGDGCD

To tune into DGDGCD from standard tuning, lower your first and sixth (top and bottom) strings a whole step from E to D. Next, lower your fifth string from A to G. Finally, raise your second string a half step from B to C. Your first and sixth strings should match your third string. To tune into DGDGCD from DADGAD, simply lower your fifth string one whole step to G and raise your second two and a half steps from A to D.

Tablature

Tablature is an early form of musical notation which has long been superseded by the (to most) more familiar modern staff notation. In recent years, however, tablature has become very popular for transcribing instrumental music for a number of instruments, including dulcimer, five-string banjo, and guitar. Modern guitar tablature is descended from lute tablature, which included rhythmic as well as melodic information. Generally speaking, modern guitar tablature contains no rhythmic indications and is therefore usually printed in conjunction with standard musical transcription.

The lines in tablature represent not scale positions but the strings themselves, which are presented in pitch order from the lowest (6th string) to the highest (1st string). The name of each string usually appears at the beginning of the transcription. The tablature lines for DADGAD are:

```
D ——— 1st string ——————————————————————
A ——— 2nd string ——————————————————————
G ——— 3rd string ——————————————————————
D ——— 4th string ——————————————————————
A ——— 5th string ——————————————————————
D ——— 6th string ——————————————————————
```

For DGDGCD they are:

```
D ——— 1st string ——————————————————————
C ——— 2nd string ——————————————————————
G ——— 3rd string ——————————————————————
D ——— 4th string ——————————————————————
G ——— 5th string ——————————————————————
D ——— 6th string ——————————————————————
```

Numbers on the lines indicate which frets should be played (*not* which fingers should be used), with 0 representing an open string. Play only those strings on which numbers appear. In the example below, only the top four strings are sounded, with three open strings (D, A, and D) and one fretted string (G, at the second fret).

```
D ——— 0 ——————————————————————
A ——— 0 ——————————————————————
G ——— 2 ——————————————————————
D ——— 0 ——————————————————————
A ————————————————————————————
D ————————————————————————————
```

In addition to indicating notes, tablature can also supply important information about technical aspects of performance. Letters above the numbers represent such information as the occurrence of a pull-off, a hammer-on, or a slide. Note in the examples below that a slide between notes is also indicated by a diagonal line connecting the notes, while a hammer-on or a pull-off is always indicated with a tie:

S = Slide
H = Hammer-on
P = Pull-off

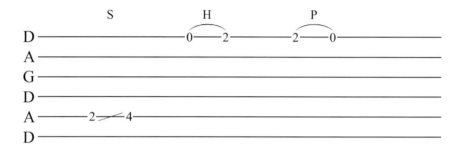

A wavy line beside a chord indicates that the notes of the chord are to be played consecutively rather than simultaneously:

In my transcriptions I include my own symbol *B*, which stands for "brush." By brush I mean a movement in which two adjacent strings are sounded simultaneously with a single upward stroke (i.e., from treble to bass strings).

Ornamentation

One of the most frequently used ornaments in Irish music is the double grace note. In this ornament, two grace notes precede the ornamented note. Rhythmically, this ornament is actually played like a triplet, but standard notation makes it clear which are the melody notes and which the grace notes.

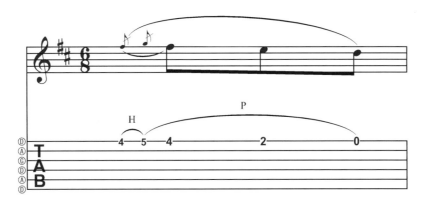

The roll is another extremely common ornament in Irish music. Again, standard notation doesn't convey the rhythmic features of this ornament particularly well, but it does give the best indication of the actual melody. The roll is not played in precise time, but can be delayed to varying degrees.

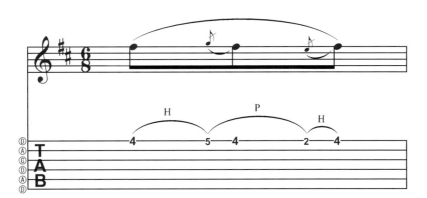

The "pseudo roll" is my name for an ornament which approximates the rhythm of an actual roll but includes only four instead of five notes. I use this ornament only on open strings.

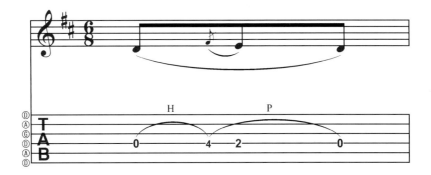

Key Signatures

Many tunes in the Irish and Breton traditions are not in either what we now call the major or minor keys, but in other scales or modes, especially the Mixolydian mode (essentially a major, or Ionian, scale with a flattened seventh) and the Dorian mode (a minor, or Aeolian, scale with a flattened seventh). For the sake of convenience, I have notated these in major or minor keys, with accidentals to compensate for variant scale steps.

Capo Use

One of the advantages of open tunings is the ability to obtain rich-sounding chords with relatively simple chord positions. The keys most easily played in DADGAD are D and (to a lesser degree) G and A; in DGDGCD, G is the principal key. To play in other keys demands the use of barre and other more complicated chord positions which often prevent the guitarist from exploiting the melodic potential, the open strings, and the sustained notes so characteristic of the tunings. For this reason most open-tunings players use the capo to play in less accessible keys—especially when playing melodically, as with dance tunes, when it is usually desirable to play out of the home position (D in DADGAD and G in DGCGCD). I have indicated capo positions for each of the tunes transcribed in this book, but feel free to experiment with these—especially those for the songs, which I have simply transcribed in the keys which suit my own vocal range.

Fingerings

I have indicated a number of fingerings for the left hand in the standard notation of the following tunes and songs, using Arabic numerals to represent the first through the fourth fingers. I have also supplied suggestions for right-hand fingerings above the tablature. With his permission, I have adopted guitarist Mark Hanson's right-hand finger symbols, which are essentially English versions of the Spanish symbols used in classical repertoire:

t = thumb
i = index finger
m = middle finger
r = ring finger

Note: Where possible, I have indicated the true value of sustained notes in the standard notation of the melodies and accompaniments in this book. Frequently, however, especially in the case of higher voices—or where the occurrence of several sustained notes (usually from open strings) would make strict transcriptions overly cluttered—I have simply indicated the melodic value of the note and trusted to the guitarist's common sense to supply the rest.

The guitarist may also notice cases where I have indicated a noted string when I could have played an open one. My own rationale for noting in such instances is to give the passage more melodic "ballast," or, in some cases, simply because it comes naturally. If so desired, obviously, you may play an open string instead of a noted one.

Chord Charts

The chord charts I have provided are not comprehensive, but they include most of the chords used in this book. Note that if I have provided a chart with a chord shape in one key (with or without a capo), it will not be represented in other keys that depend upon the capoed position. Also, the notation *nr* (an abbreviation for *no root*) after a chord name indicates that the root of the chord (derived from the overall harmonic context rather from the notes of the "chord" as given) is not present.

Acknowledgements

I would like to thank Gilles le Bigot, Fred Boyce, Johnny Moynihan, Phil Cooper, and Jake Schumacher for allowing me to use their compositions and arrangements. I also wish to thank Federico Marincola for proofreading the music.

Dedication

I dedicate this book to the memory of the late Mícheál Ó Domhnaill. Ar dheis Dé go raibh a anam uasal.

Used by permission

The Lark on the Strand

"The Lark on the Strand" (also known as "The Lark in the Strand") was recorded in 1922 by Michael Coleman and Michael Walsh along with "The Primrose Vale." Because the original 78 record only listed the title "The Lark on the Strand," the tunes have often appeared under each other's names. The Chieftains recorded it on their first album in 1963, which may have led to its resurgence in popularity since that time. I first heard this beguiling jig a number of years ago, played by Tullamore whistle player Val Hughes, while sheltering from the rain in a doorway in Miltown Malbay, County Clare.

Capo: 5th Fret   Trad./Arr. Julie Henigan

Variations

15

Jésaïg

This haunting melody was composed by Breton guitarist Gilles le Bigot. Paddy Keenan, the renowned Irish piper, brought it to greater attention when he recorded it on his album *Poirt an Phíobaire* (Gael-Linn 099) in 1983. Le Bigot subsequently recorded it on *Tunes for America*, a tape that he and accordionist Serge Desaunay made for a tour in the United States in the mid-eighties. Since then Le Bigot has performed with many Breton groups, including Kornog, Skolvan, and Barzaz, and has collaborated with both Breton and Irish musicians, including Soïg Siberil (another noted Breton solo guitarist), Gerry O'Connor and Eithne Ní Uallacháin. Keeping your fingers in chord positions will facilitate the performance of the tune.

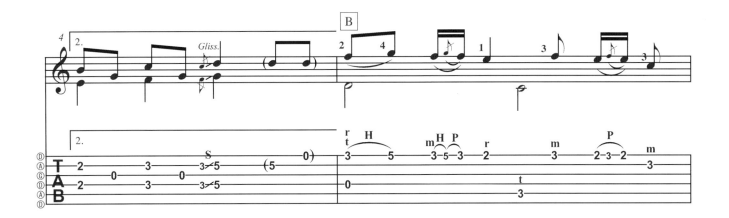

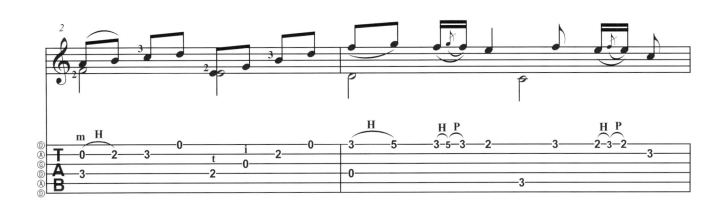

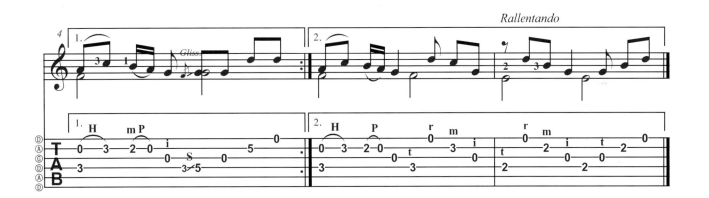

Variation
A4.2

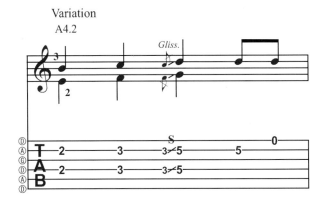

Old Hag, You Have Killed Me

This jig, also known as "Oh, Hag, You Have Killed Me," appears on a well-known album of the same name recorded by the Bothy Band in 1976. My setting of this tune features both the roll and the pseudo-roll. For a fuller explanation of the roll and the pseudo-roll, see the section on ornamentation in the introduction. This tune is in D Mixolydian.

Mother Broomstick.

Trad./Arr. Julie Henigan

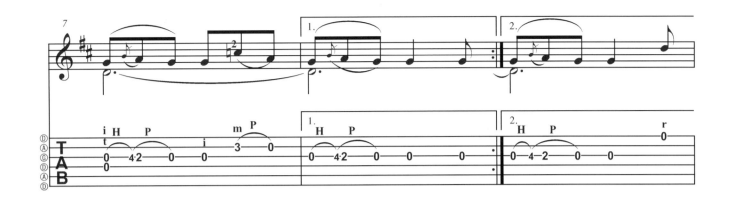

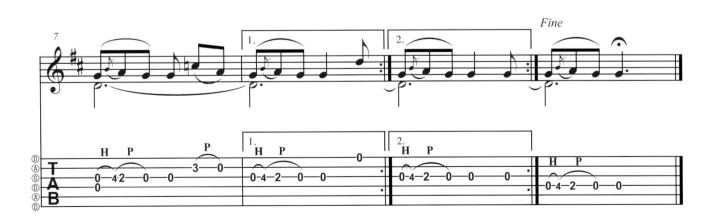

Boland's Favorite

The jig, which probably originated in Italy, may be the oldest surviving form of Irish dance music. Historically, the jig has taken various forms, but in modern Irish music three forms, the single jig, the double jig, and the slip jig, have come to predominate. By far the most common of these is the double jig, played in 6/8 time, with each part typically consisting of seven bars of two triplets each, followed by an eighth bar containing a triplet and a quarter note.

As a dance, the solo jig was characterized in Elizabethan times as "full of leapings" and (especially in Ireland) was associated with "stepping" or "beating out intricate movements with the feet" (see *The New Grove Dictionary of Music and Musicians*). As early as the end of the seventeenth century, however, the jig had come to be associated with Ireland, where it received its greatest elaboration. Danced solo or with a partner as a "step dance," the early Irish jig was also characterized by energetic up and down movements, as well as by either "battering" steps for men or more feminine "shuffling" steps for women. (See Breandán Breathnach's *Folk Music and Dances of Ireland*.)

I know little about this jig, although it has been recorded by both the Chieftains and by Grey Larson and Malcolm Dalglish on their album *Thunderhead*. It was popular among the Irish musicians in the North Carolina Triangle area when I lived there in the mid-1980s. In D Mixolydian.

Trad./Arr. Julie Henigan

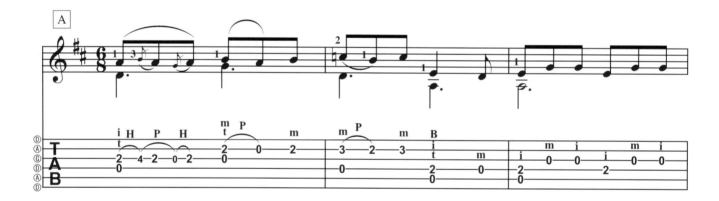

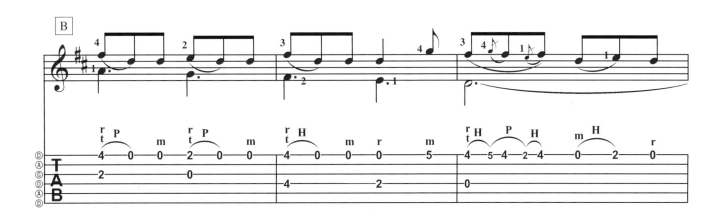

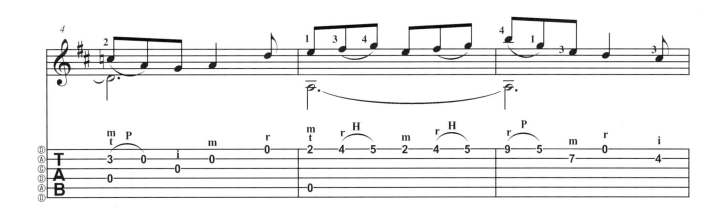

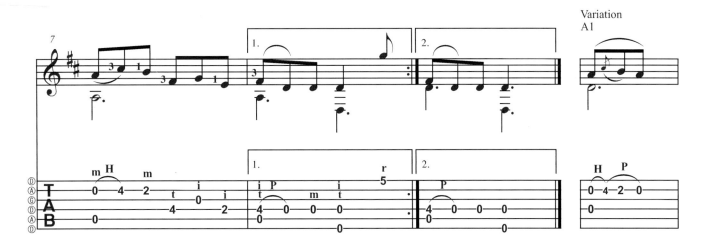

Variation
A1

The Plains of Boyle

According to The New Grove Dictionary of Music and Musicians, the hornpipe (historically a solo dance form) has existed in Scotland and Wales "immemorially, and in England since at least the sixteenth century." There it eventually changed from syncopated 3/2 to 4/4 time. The modern hornpipe is distinguished from the reel, also in 4/4 time, by having two strong accents per measure (as opposed to one), with three accented quarter notes in the final bar of each part. It is also notable for its dotted rhythm: Irish hornpipes should swing. Although it is usually not notated, this rhythmic trait is always present in performance to varying degrees. I have therefore transcribed the following hornpipes with dotted notes, which, while not a strictly accurate representation of the rhythm (the value of the dotted notes as I play them, for example, is closer to 2:3 than 3:4), at least indicates that the notes are not of uniform length.

"The Plains of Boyle" ranks No. 7 in the "Top Ten Hornpipes of the Century" on Irishtuneinfo.com. Its popularity surely stems from the irresistible lilt of its phrasing. The great Irish guitarist and singer Mick Hanly recorded a marvelous version of the tune in DADGAD tuning on his 1980 Mulligan release *As I Went over Blackwater*. This is my arrangement.

A Fidler   Hornpipe

24

Pol Ha'penny

The first version of this hornpipe I learned was a lesser-known variant played by Julia Clifford of Lisheen, Gneevguilla, County Kerry. This is the more popular version of the tune, which dates back to at least the time of collector Edward Bunting (1773-1843). Guitarist Mark Simos has recorded a lovely rendition of this tune on *The Starry Lane to Monaghan*. This tune is in G Mixolydian, notated in the key of C. The ringing or sustained notes of the open strings give this tune a particularly harp-like quality.

Capo: 5th Fret

Trad./Arr. Julie Henigan

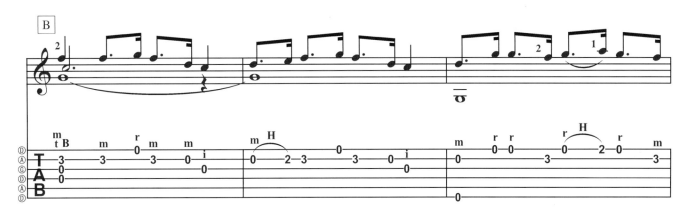

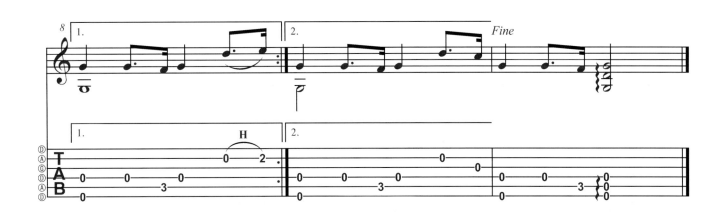

The Puncheon Floor

This reel has (to my ears) a very New England sound—although it has cropped up in Michigan, as well. There is also a "breakdown" of the same name, but it seems to be unrelated to the tune I print here, which I learned from fellow guitarist Phil Cooper. Note that the A part of this tune is in G, while the B part is in D.

Trad./Arr. Phil Cooper & Julie Henigan

The Whale's Ear

When I was living in North Carolina in the 1980s, I and a group of local musicians gathered around a campfire to celebrate the birthday of our friend Tríona Ní Dhomhnaill. When another friend learned the reason for the gathering, he ran to his truck and promptly returned with a gift for Tríona: an unusual-looking fossil, which, he informed us, was the petrified inner ear of a baby whale. I later composed this polka to commemorate the event.

© 1986 Julie Henigan

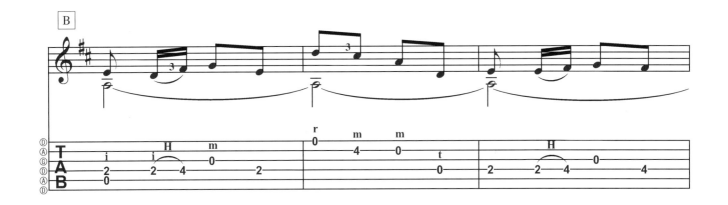

Whales in the Sea
Gods Voice Obey

Hoban's Hill

Mike Hoban was a stone mason, horse breeder, and gifted accordion player from County Mayo, Ireland. He and his wife Monica made central Missouri their home for many years, and there he influenced and mentored a number of aspiring Irish musicians. In October 1993, Mike and Monica hosted a reunion for these friends—by then scattered throughout the country—at their farm near Columbia. The music, friendship, and beautiful autumn scenery made it an extraordinarily memorable weekend. I wrote this untraditional-sounding waltz in an attempt to capture the peaceful mood of the first balmy evening when we played outside and watched the sunset. Mike was also an exceptional tune composer; his reel "The Foal" (known also as "The Well-Bred Foal" and "Mike Hoban's") can be heard on the Altan's *The Blue Idol*, Paddy O'Brien's *Tune Collection*, Lunasa's *Sé*, and *Snug in the Blanket* with Paddy O'Brien, Jamie Gans, and Dáithí Sproule.

Photograph by Julie Henigan

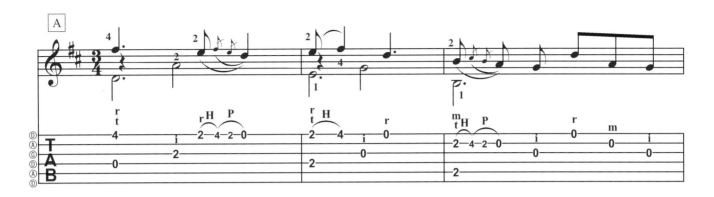

Variations

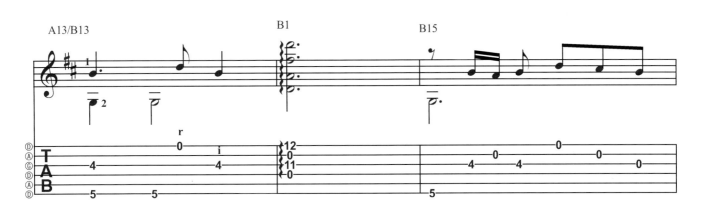

Soir et Matin

This delightful waltz was composed by Gilles le Bigot. I first heard it on his and Serge Desaunay's *Tunes for America*. I seem to have "reinterpreted" Le Bigot's tune slightly, but I hope not to its detriment. In this tune, you will need to bend and release the high B in measure A5 a half-step (up to C and back to B). I have indicated this action in the tablature, using a *B* to stand for *bend* and an *R* for *release*.

Capo: 5th Fret

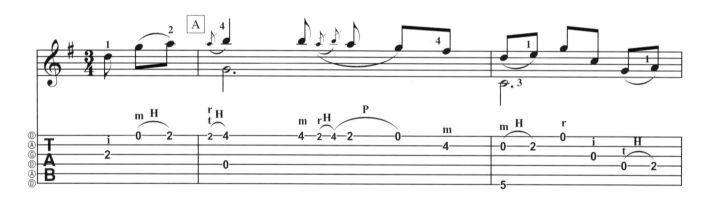

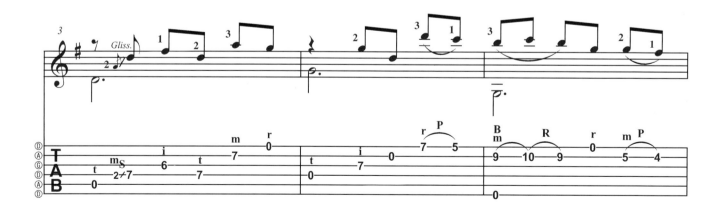

36

Variations

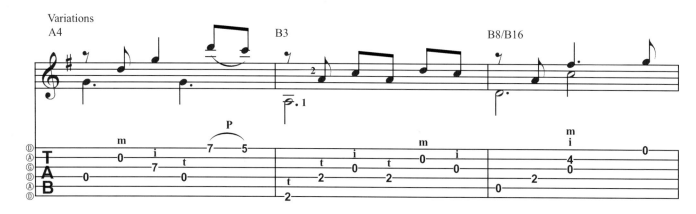

Caoineadh na Réalta (The Lament of the Stars)

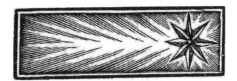

The first time I heard my friend Fred Boyce (herpetologist and banjo-player *extraordinaire*) play this enchanting tune, I knew I had to set it for the guitar. The tune had no name, so Fred allowed me to give it this fanciful title, suggested by the air's plaintive melody.

40

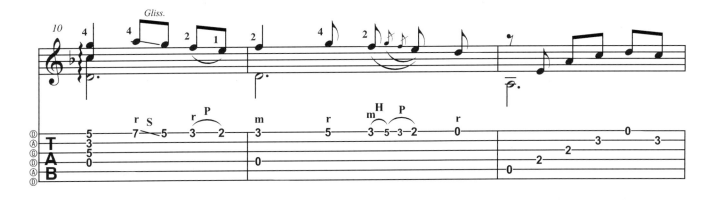

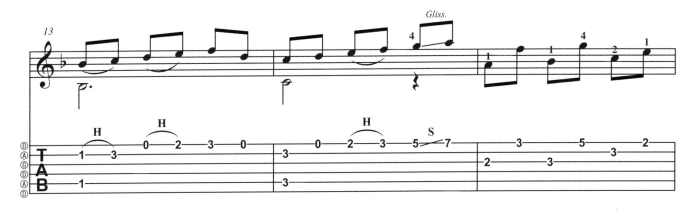

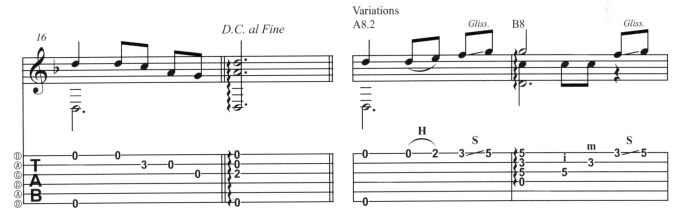

Adieu, My Lovely Nancy

One of a number of departed sailor songs printed on ballad sheets in the late eighteenth and early nineteenth centuries, "Adieu, My Lovely Nancy" (also known as "The Sailor's Farewell," "Swansea Town," and "The Holy Ground") has been collected in England, Ireland, Australia, Canada, and the United States. I learned this version from the Max Hunter Collection. Hunter was a traveling salesman and amateur folksong collector from Springfield, Missouri, who amassed an impressive number of field recordings from the Missouri and Arkansas Ozarks. When I was a teenager, I learned many songs from the cassette tapes of his collection that were housed in the Springfield Public Library. They are now available on-line (maxhunter.missouristate.edu).

Hunter recorded this song in 1959 from Bertha Lauderdale, of Fayetteville, Arkansas. She had learned the song from her grandfather, who, in turn, had learned it from his grandmother when "he was a young child in Ireland." Certainly her version sounds very Irish—enough for traditional Donegal singer Neilí Ní Dhomhnaill to want me to record it for her when I was meant to be collecting songs from *her*. Since I recorded the song on *American Stranger*, Altan, Jeff Davis, Nancy Conescu, Gerald Trimble, and Pete Coe have all added it to their repertoires. I wish Bertha were alive today to see how many people her grandfather's song has inspired.

Capo: 5th Fret

Trad./Arr. Julie Henigan

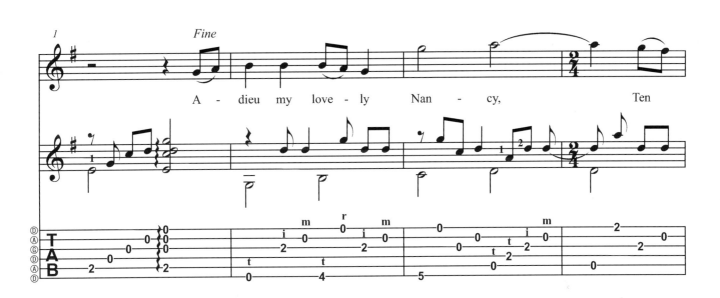

43

own true love,   I'll be   think-ing, dear, of   you.   Will you

Instrumental

D.C. al Fine

44

Variations (Accompaniment)

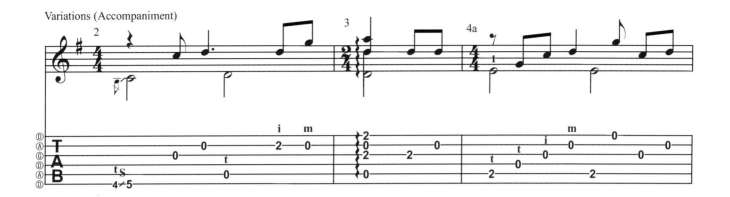

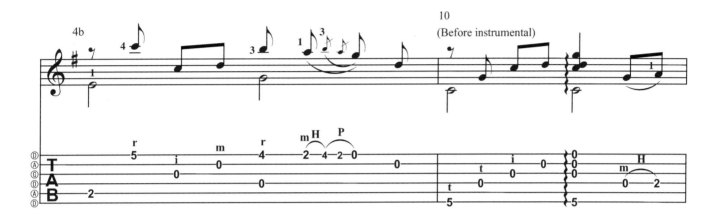

Adieu, my lovely Nancy,
Ten thousand times adieu,
I'll be thinking of my own true love,
I'll be thinking, dear, of you.

Will you change a ring with me, my love,
Will you change a ring with me?
It will be a token of our love
When I am far at sea.

When I am far away, my love,
And you know not where I am,
Love letters I will write to you
From every foreign strand.

When the farmer boys return at night,
They will tell their girls fine tales
Of all that they've been doing
All day out in the fields.

Of the wheat and hay that they've cut down,
Sure, it's all that they can do,
While we poor jolly, jolly hearts of oak
Must plough the seas all through.

And when we return again, my love,
To our own dear native shore,
Fine stories we will tell to you,
How we ploughed the oceans o'er.

And we'll make the alehouses to ring,
And the taverns they will roar,
And when our money it is all gone,
Sure, we'll go to sea for more.

I Loved You More

The slide, usually classed as a kind of jig and often notated in 12/8 time, is characterized by a rhythm of alternating quarter and eighth notes, with a feel of four beats per measure (as opposed to the two of double jigs in 6/8 time). The A and B parts frequently end with two strongly accented dotted eighth notes. Slides are particularly popular in Counties Cork and Kerry, where they are favored by dancers because of their lively and infectious long-short rhythm.

This catchy slide is the composition of the fine Missouri accordion player Jake Schumacher, although I think the variation in the B part was likely contributed by our mutual friend Dan Leonard.

Capo: 5th Fret

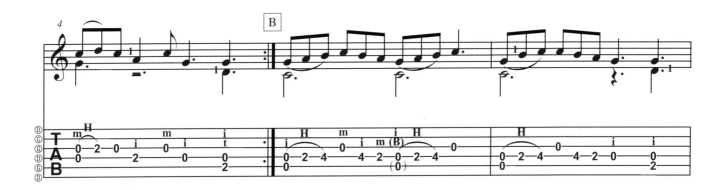

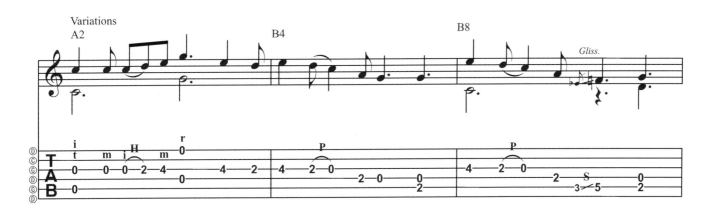

The Homesick Hornpipe

I came up with this hornpipe while (apparently) trying to remember the start of "The Fairies' Hornpipe," whose first phrase it resembles. It then takes off into something else entirely. The title is a play on "The Homebrew Hornpipe," a tune very much associated with legendary tin whistle player Micho Russell.

Capo: 5th Fret

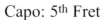

Love, Will You Marry Me?

Also known as "Some Say The Devil Is Dead," "Jenny Will You Marry Me," "Johnny Will You Marry Me," "The Braes of Mar," and "The Devil's Highland Fling," this tune is an example of a dance form known as a "fling," or "highland fling," which in turn is often identified with the "highland Schottische." Related to both the reel and the hornpipe, this form is distinguished from both by its consistent use of eight- (as opposed to sixteen-) bar parts; dotted rhythms (which in the Scottish tunes often involve the use of the Scottish "snap," in which the patterns of long and short notes are regularly alternated); and by a strong accent on the first beat of each measure. Among the better-known flings in the Irish tradition are "Green Grow the Rushes O," "The Primrose Lass," "The Keel Row," and "Stirling Castle." In Ireland this tune is associated with several different sets of words, including:

Some say the devil is dead, the devil is dead, the devil is dead,
Some say the devil is dead, and buried in Killarney.
More say he rose again, more say he rose again,
More say he rose again, and joined the British Army.

One version of the tune, performed with the lyrics, "Johnny, Will You Marry Me," was recorded by Dan Sullivan's Shamrock band, a prolific Boston-based Irish dance band that flourished in the 1920s and '30s and featured Murty Rabbett on vocals. Johnny Moynihan learned the song from one of these recordings, and, after altering the title to "Love, Will You Marry Me" and "reconstructing" the lyrics of the song, recorded it with De Danaan on *Selected Jigs, Reels and Songs*. He says he also seems to have "taken liberties" with the melody, a common enough phenomenon in traditional music.

There are several spots in this tune where you may choose to brush a bass or middle voice note with your index finger, to play it with your thumb, or to omit it altogether. For simplicity's sake, I have not notated sustained or ringing open strings. Keeping your fingers in chord shapes for this song will simplify its execution.

Capo: 5th Fret

Trad./Arr. Johnny Moynihan & Julie Henigan

Love, will you mar - ry me, mar - ry me, mar - ry me, Love, will you mar - ry me and

take me out of dan - ger? No, I won't mar - ry you, mar - ry you, mar - ry you,

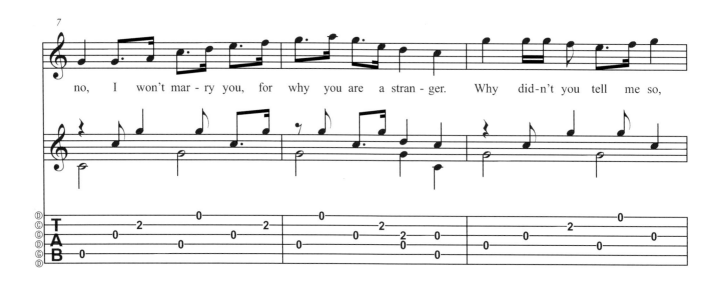

no, I won't mar - ry you, for why you are a stran - ger. Why did - n't you tell me so,

52

Why did-n't you tell me so? Why did-n't you tell me so be - fore you done the harm?

What harm did I do? What harm did I do? What harm did I do but roll you in me arms?

Variation
2nd verse

D.C. al Fine

How would I tell you so, For if I did, there is-n't a doubt I ne - ver would have gained you.

"Love, will you marry me, marry me, marry me,
Love, will you marry me and take me out of danger?"
"No, I won't marry you, marry you, marry you,
No, I won't marry you, for why you are a stranger."
"Why didn't you tell me so, why didn't you tell me so,
Why didn't you tell me so before you done the harm?"
"What harm did I do, what harm did I do,
What harm did I do but roll you in my arms?"

"Love, will you marry me, marry me, marry me,
Love, will you marry me and take me out of danger?"
"No, I won't marry you, marry you, marry you,
No, I won't marry you, for why you are a stranger."
"Why didn't you tell me so, why didn't you tell me so,
Why didn't you tell me so, what the devil ailed you?"
"How could I tell you so, how would I tell so,
For if I did, there isn't a doubt I never would ha' gained you."

54

The Trip O'er the Mountain

According to folksong scholar John Moulden, the lyrics of this delightful elopement song were written during the first half of the nineteenth century by Hugh McWilliams, a schoolmaster and poet from Glenavey, County Antrim. (See Moulden's *Songs of Hugh McWilliams, Schoolmaster, 1831*.) McWilliams appears to have composed a number of songs that have since become popular in the Irish song tradition, including "Trip o'er the Mountain," "When a Man's in Love He Feels No Cold," and "The Lass among the Heather." This particular song exists in a number of versions. Mine is based principally on that performed by the superb County Antrim singer Len Graham, whose primary source was the great Eddie Butcher, of Magilligan, County Derry. Like Graham, I've made a few minor alterations based on versions found in print.

It happened to be on a moonshiny night when I first took a notion to marry;
I lifted my hat and my staff in my hand, and I seemed for to be in a hurry.
When I came to the dwelling where oft-times I'd been, my heart it rejoiced when I viewed this fair dame;
I lifted the latch and I bade her good e'en, sayin' "Will you come over the mountain"?

"Oh, what foolish notion's come into your head, still, I'm glad for to see you so merry.
It's twelve by the clock and the old folks in bed; speak low or my mammy she'll hear ye."
"Well, if it is jesting, it's jesting that's true; I've courted a year, and I think that should do;
So this very night I will marry with you, if you'll venture with me o'er the mountain.

"Oh, then, you're in earnest," she said with a smile, "Kind Providence be my director."
"I've love in my bosom I ne'er will deny"; this sentence did seem to affect her.
"I'm using no magic, no art, nor no spell, I've a true honest heart and I love you right well;
So, if you'll consent and my parents don't tell, we'll both make our way o'er the mountain.

"Oh, no, my wee laddie, I'll stay as I am, for I think it is fitter and better."
I lifted my hat and my staff in my hand, saying, "I'll soon put an end to this matter."
"Stop, stop, bonnie laddie, 'til I get my shoes"; my heart it rejoiced when I heard the glad news.
She ran to the door, saying, "I hope you'll excuse: I'd love to go over the mountain."

The moon and the stars 'luminated the sky, and the morning star brightly was shining,
As me and my darling our journey pursued 'til we came to the altar of Hymen.
Between fiddling and dancing we spent the whole day, and the fear of marriage soon faded
 away,
But often unto my wee darling I say, "Do you rue going over the mountain?"

"Oh, no, my dearie, oh, why should I rue, sure, I took the advice of my laddie,
And now that I'm over the mountain with you, I regard not the frowns of my daddy."
So, let this be a warning to all pretty maids: slip out with your lad with the old folks in bed,
And don't be afraid your fair charmer to wed, but think on the lass o'er the mountain.

Capo: 7th Fret

Trad./Arr. Julie Henigan

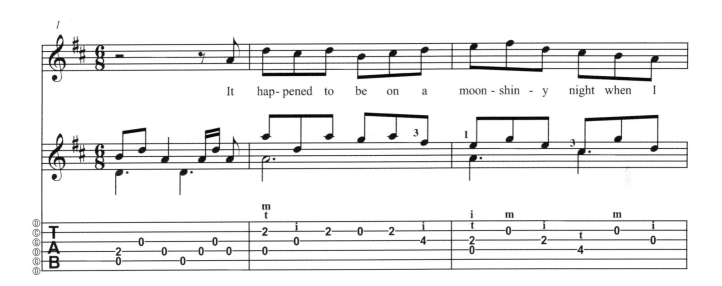

It hap-pened to be on a moon-shin - y night when I

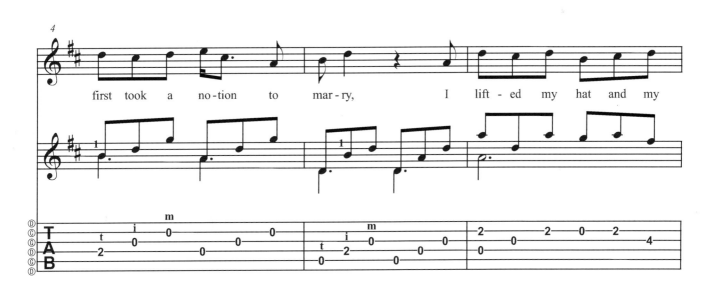

first took a no-tion to mar-ry, I lift - ed my hat and my

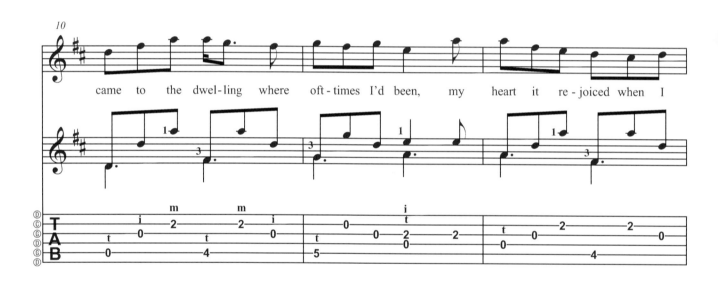

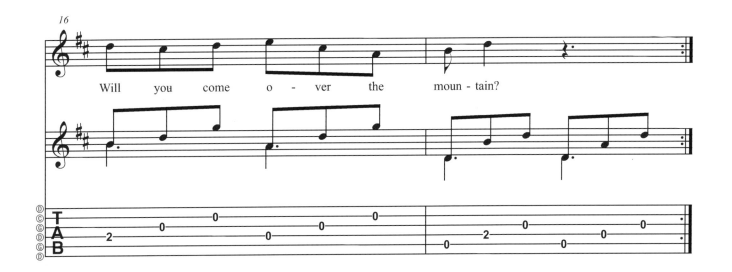

Will you come o - ver the moun - tain?

Discography/Bibliography

This list of recordings and books is not meant to be comprehensive, but rather to give the reader a sampling from the world of open tunings—and of DADGAD and DGDGCD in particular. The recordings were chosen with a bias toward fingerstyle guitar; some are of solo performances, while others feature the guitar as an accompanying instrument. The repertoire ranges from blues to New Age. I have also included books from which I have drawn for musical history and background information on individual tunes and songs.

Recordings:

D'Agostino, Peppino. *Acoustic Spirit*, Shanachie 96002 (originals in DADGAD).

Bensusan, Pierre. *Près de Paris*, Rounder 3023 (traditional French and Irish music in DADGAD—a highly influential album); *Solilaï*, Rounder 3068 (originals with a New Age feel).

Carthy, Martin. *The Collection*, Green Linnet 1136; *Life and Limb*, Green Linnet 3052 (with fiddler Dave Swarbrick). Carthy, one of the guitar giants of the English folk scene, developed a number of his own distinctive tunings from DADGAD. He has also occasionally used DGDGCD.

Cooper, Phil. *The Northland Waltz: Celtic Tunes Arranged for Guitar*, Phil Cooper 2118 (primarily traditional Scottish tunes, played solo and with other instruments, mostly in DADGAD).

Evans, Dave, Duck Baker, Dan ar Bras, *Irish Reels, Jigs, Airs and Hornpipes*, Shanachie-CD97011/C97011 (accompanying tab booklet available from Shanachie). Features tunes played in a variety of open tunings by superb guitarists from England, the U.S., and Brittany.

Graham, Davey. *The Complete Guitarist*, Kicking Mule 138; *Dance for Two People*, Kicking Mule 161; *Folk Blues and All Points in Between*, SFM-CD48. Three albums by the man who first popularized DADGAD.

Hedges, Michael. *Aerial Boundaries*, Windham Hill 1032; *Beyond Boundaries: Guitar Solos* (Windham Hill 01934). Prolific original New Age composer-guitarist.

Hanly, Mick. *A Kiss in the Morning Early; As I Went Over Blackwater* (traditional Irish songs and tunes). Hanly uses DADGAD to great effect in both instrumentals and song accompaniments.

Henigan, Julie. *American Stranger*, Waterbug 035.

Jansch, Bert. *The Best of Bert Jansch*, Shanachie 99004. Jansch was heavily influenced by Davey Graham and collaborated with John Renbourn both as a duo and in the folk-rock group Pentangle.

Jones, Nic. *Penguin Eggs*, Shanachie 79090; *Unearthed*, Mollie Music MMCD02/03; *Game, Set, and Match*, Topic TSCD566 (traditional English and Irish songs and instrumentals). Another English guitar master, Jones used open tunings inventively and with great flair; though he tended to prefer tunings in G and C, his approach to arranging traditional music for the guitar is edifying, to say the least.

Le Bigot, Gilles. *Skolvan*, Keltia Musique 46 (eclectic Breton ensemble). Le Bigot is an exquisite Breton DADGAD guitarist and composer who has performed with Breton groups Barzaz, Kornog, Skolvan, and Galorn, as well as with Caliana (also featuring Gerry O'Connor, Niamh Parsons, and Michel Sikiotakis). He also appears on *Lá Lugh* (Claddagh 4CCF29) with Gerry O'Connor and Eithne Ní Uallacháin.

Masure, Philip, *Piccard & Masure: Webbesnaren*, Wild Boar Music WBM21012. The Flemish Masure specializes in DADGAD and has recorded with Belgian bands Orion, Floes, and Urban Trad, as well as with Irish fiddler Aidan Burke and multi-instrumentalist Guido Piccard.

Ó Domhnaill, Mícheál. *Portland*, Green Linnet 1041 (with fiddler Kevin Burke); *The Best of the Bothy Band*, Green Linnet 3001; *Shadow of Time*, Windham-Hill 11130 (with Irish/New Age group Nightnoise). Ó Domhnaill's accompaniments for traditional Irish songs and dance music have been highly influential.

Quemener, Nicolas, *Faoi Bhláth*, Folkroads 022 (with fiddler Dave Sheridan and flute player Ciaran Somers). The highly regarded Quemener has also performed and recorded with both Irish, Belgian, and Breton groups, including Arcady, Orion, Kornog, and Skeduz.

Renbourn, John. *A Maid That's Deep in Love*, Shanachie 79066; *The Enchanted Garden*, Shanachie 79074. Renbourn was influenced by Davey Graham, collaborated with Bert Jansch, and has probably exploited early music more than any other British folk guitarist.

Siberil, Soïg. *Guitares Celtiques*, Sony Music GRI19060.2; *Digor*, Gwerz Pladden 005; *Ar Seizh Avel: On Seven Winds*, Green Linnet 1062 (with the Breton band Kornog). Siberil is one of the leading Breton exponents of DADGAD, which he uses for both accompaniments and solo pieces.

Simos, Mark. *The Starry Lane to Monaghan*, Whinstone Discs 001 (with flute-player Fintan Vallely); *Crazy Faith*, Devachan Music DEV-CD4347. Simos is a superb accompanist and soloist. He can also be heard on Eileen Iver's *Fresh Takes*, Green Linnet 1075.

Simpson, Martin. *Leaves of Life*, Shanachie 97008 (guitar solos; free tab book available); *When I Was on Horseback*, Shanachie 97016; and *True Stories*, Compass B002M9FYGW (songs and instrumentals).

Dáithí Sproule, *A Heart Made of Glass*, Green Linnet 1123 (songs and guitar solos); *Is It Yourself*, Shanachie 29015 (with fiddler James Kelly and accordion-player Paddy O'Brien); *Trian*, Flying Fish 586 (with fiddler Liz Carroll and accordion-player Billy McComiskey); *Local Ground*, Narada 724387592728 (with Altan); and others. While early on he worked with Mícheál Ó Domhnaill in Skara Brae, Sproule developed his own distinctive and harmonically rich approach to DADGAD, both in his accompaniments and in his solo pieces.

Surette, David. *Back Roads*, ONE 03. This album features a number of different instruments, but includes several Breton and Irish tunes on guitar. Available through Ossian USA, 118 Beck Rd., Loudon, NH 03301-1119.

Thompson, Richard. *Guitar/Vocal*, Hannibal 4413; *Pour Down Like Silver* (with former wife Linda), Island; *Strict Tempo*, Hannibal 4409 (guitar solos); *Small Town Romance*, Hannibal 1316; and many more. Known for his work with folk-rock band Fairport Convention and with former wife Linda, Richard Thompson has used DADGAD extensively throughout his career, from his early folk-rock days to the present.

Books:

Baker, Duck. *The Salutation: A Collection of Christmas Carols from England, Ireland, Scotland, Sweden, Germany, Italy and France.* Mel Bay Publications, 2001. (Features two tunes in DADGAD).

Bensusan, Pierre. *DADGAD Music: Compositions from "Spices" and "Wu Wei."* John August/Mel Bay Publications, 1996.

Breathnach, Brendán. *Folk Music and Dances of Ireland.* Cork: Mercier Press, 1971.

Grossman, Stefan. *British Fingerpicking Guitar* and *Blarney Pilgrim*, Mel Bay Publications, 1990.

Grossman, Stefan. *Fingerstyle Guitar: New Dimensions and Explorations.* Mel Bay Publications, 1995. (Includes arrangements by John Renbourn, Martin Carthy, Dave Evans, Martin Simpson, and others.)

Grossman, Stefan, Duck Baker, El McMeen. *Mel Bay's Complete Celtic Fingerstyle Guitar Book.* Mel Bay Publications, 1995.

Hanson, Mark. *The Complete Book of Alternative Tunings.* West Linn, OR: Accent on Music, 1995. (Available from Accent on Music, 19363 Willamette Drive, #252, West Linn, OR 97078.)

Hanson, Mark. "Exploring Open Tunings: An Introduction to DADGAD." *Acoustic Guitar* November/December, 1994.

Henigan, Julie. *DADGAD Tuning.* Mel Bay Publications, 1999.

McQuaid, Sarah. *The Irish DADGAD Guitar Book: Playing and Backing Traditional Irish Music on Open-Tuned Guitar.* Cork, Ireland: Ossian Publications, 1995.

Moulden, John. *Songs of Hugh McWilliams, Schoolmaster, 1831.* Portrush: Ulstersongs, 1993. www.scallta.com/ulstersongs.

The New Grove Dictionary of Music and Musicians, Stanley Sadie, editor. London: MacMillan Publishers Ltd., 1980.

Siberil, Soïg. *Gitar Partitions: Musique Bretonne & Celtique.* Coop Breizh, 2002; *Musique Celtique.* Coop Breizh, 1997.

Surette, David. *Down the Brae: Celtic Finger Style Guitar.* Pacific, MO: Mel Bay Publications, 1996.

Chord Charts

A	A	A	A	A/C♯

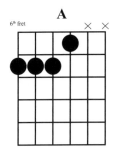 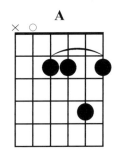 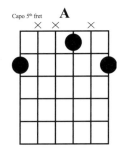 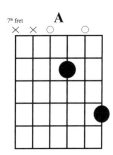 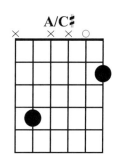

A(m)	Am	Am	Am	Am/nr

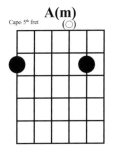 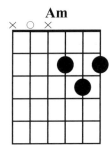 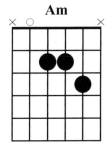 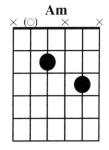 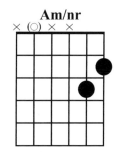

Am add2	Am add 4	Am add4/D	A7/C♯	A⁷₅

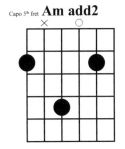 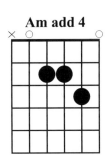 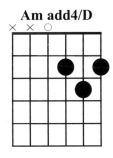 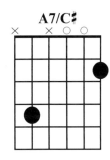 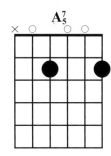

A7 add4/C♯	A modal(A5)	A modal(A5)	A modal(A5)	A modal(A5)

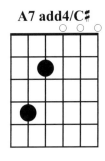 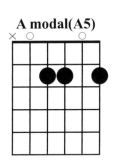 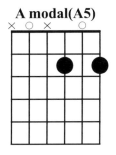 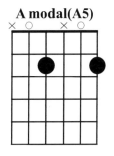 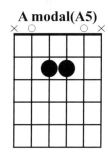

A modal(A5)	Asus4	A7sus4	Bm	Bm7 add6

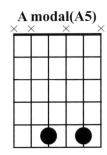 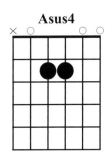 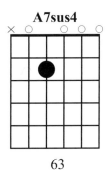 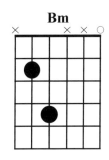 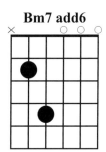

B modal(B5)   **B♭maj7**   **B♭maj7**   **B♭maj7 add6**   **B♭maj7 add6**

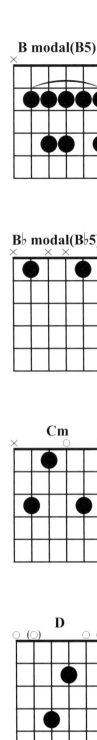 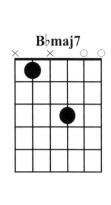 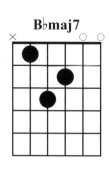 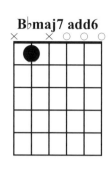 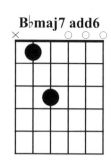

B♭ modal(B♭5)   **C**   **C**   **C add2**   **C add2**

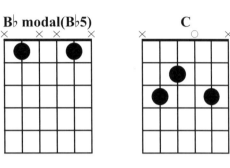 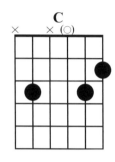 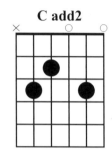 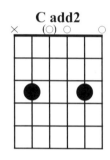

Cm   **Cm add2**   **C modal(C5)**   **C modal/D**   **C6sus2**

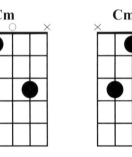 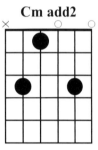 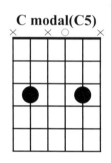 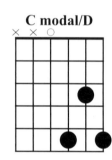 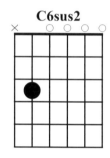

D   **D**   **D**   **D**   **D(7)/nr**

7ᵗʰ fret   Capo 5ᵗʰ fret   Capo 5ᵗʰ fret

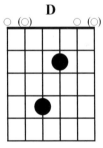 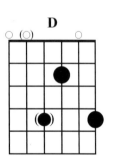 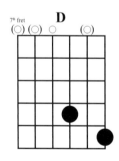 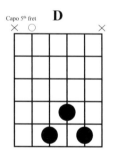 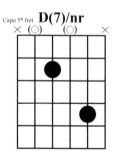

D/F♯   **D add4**   **D add4**   **D add4**   **D add4/F♯**

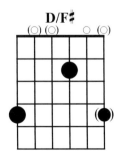 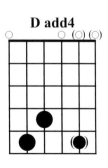 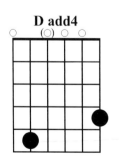 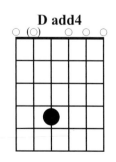 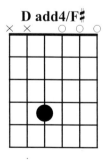

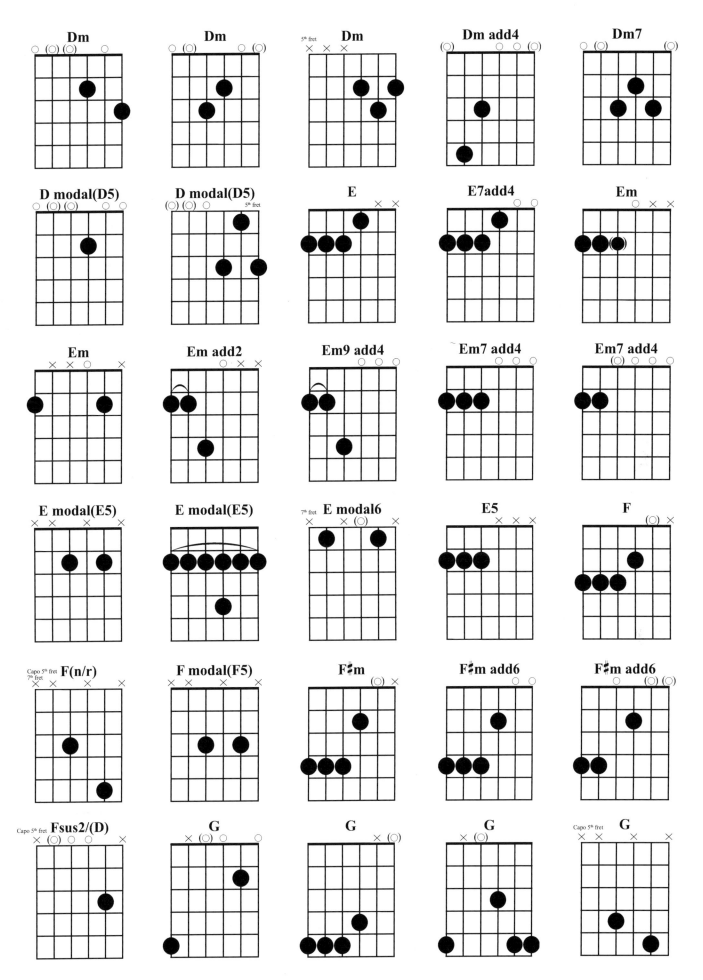

65

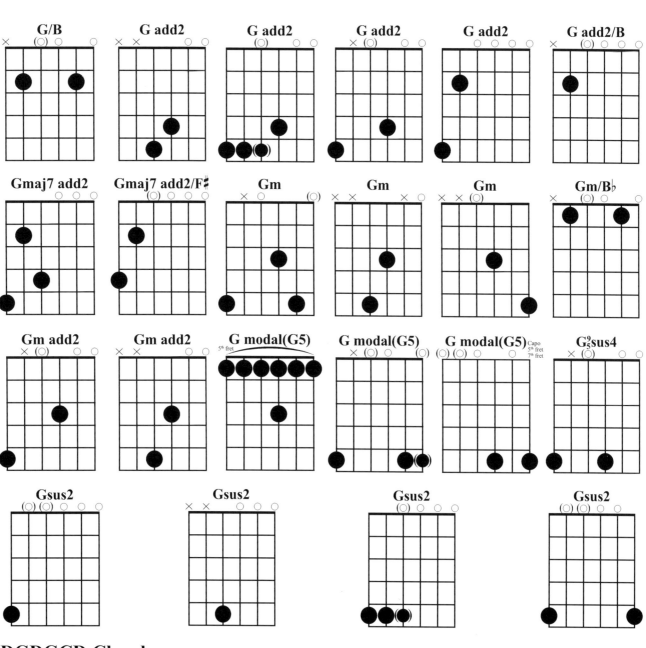

DGDGCD Chords

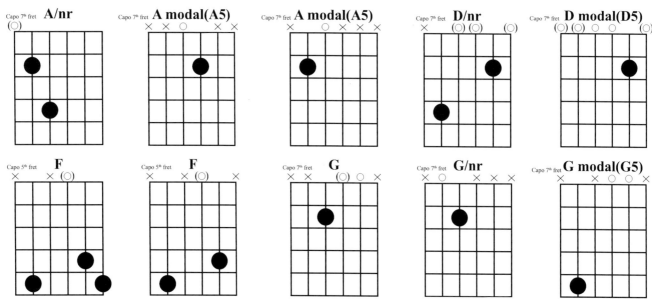

About the Author

Julie Henigan, a Missouri native, first taught herself to play guitar at the age of twelve, and later studied classical guitar and lute repertoire at Washington University in St. Louis. Her first guitar book, *DADGAD Tuning*, was published by Mel Bay in 1999. She has toured extensively in Britain, Ireland, and North America, performing traditional and original material, singing, and playing guitar, fiddle, lap dulcimer, and five-string banjo. She has lectured widely on traditional Irish and American music and has written about traditional music and culture for a variety of publications, including *The Companion to Irish Traditional Music*, *Musical Traditions Magazine*, and *The Old-Time Herald*. Julie has recorded one solo album (*American Stranger*, Waterbug 035) and is featured on *Sean-Nós cois Locha* (Cló Iar-Chonnachta CICD 162), an anthology of singers recorded at the traditional singing festival Sean-Nós Milwaukee. For further details and contact information, see www.juliehenigan.com.

Photograph by Lee Worman

Manufactured by Amazon.ca
Bolton, ON

31315676R00039